CW01108736

Home Recording 101

Creating Your Own Affordable Home Recording Studio

2nd Edition

Rake Helson

Copyright © 2014, 2015 Rach Helson LLC

All rights reserved.

In no way is it legal to reproduce, duplicate, or transmit any part of this document in either electronic means or in printed format. Recording of this publication is strictly prohibited and any storage of this document is not allowed unless with written permission from the publisher. All rights reserved.

The information provided herein is stated to be truthful and consistent, in that any liability, in terms of inattention or otherwise, by any usage or abuse of any policies, processes, or directions contained within is the solitary and utter responsibility of the recipient reader. Under no circumstances will any legal responsibility or blame be held against the publisher for any reparation, damages, or monetary loss due to the information herein, either directly or indirectly.

Respective authors own all copyrights not held by the publisher.

Legal Notice:

This book is copyright protected. This is only for personal use. You cannot amend, distribute, sell, use, quote or paraphrase any part or the content within this book without the consent of the author or copyright owner. Legal action will be pursued if this is breached.

Disclaimer Notice:

Please note the information contained within this document is for educational and entertainment purposes only. Every attempt has been made to provide accurate, up to date and reliable, complete information. No warranties of any kind are expressed or implied. Readers acknowledge that the author is not engaging in the rendering of legal, financial, medical or professional advice.

Table of Contents

Introduction ix
Essential Hardware 1
    Microphone 1
    Audio Interface 2
    Digital Keyboard 3
    Studio Monitors 4
    Headphones 5
    Cables. 6
    Computer. 6
Essential Software 7
    Audacity 8
    Adobe Audition 8
    Reaper 9
    Ableton Live 9
    Mix Vibes. 10
    Loop Labs 10
    Tactile 10
Designing the Home Recording Studio. 11
    Sound Isolation 12
    Sound Absorption. 13
    Use egg crate foams 13
    Use acoustic traps 14
Recording Tips for Various Musical Instruments 17
    How to Tune your Instruments 17
    Tuning your Drum Kit 17

    Tuning your String Instruments 19

    Basic Recording Tips – Percussion 20

    Basic Recording Tips – Acoustic Guitar 20

How to Record Music 23

    The Basics 23

    The "It Will Be Fixed During the Mix" Strategy 24

    The Eight Steps of the Process 25

Writing the Song 27

    The Traditional Technique 27

    The Modern Technique 27

    The Four Fundamental Principles of Songwriting 28

Saving a Demo Copy 33

    The Importance of the Demo Stage 33

    The Process of Recording a Demo 34

    Two Factors You Need to Consider 34

The Rehearsals 37

    How Rehearsals Influence the Recording Stage 39

    Rehearsal for the Vocalist 40

    The Things You Can Do If Rehearsals Are Not Feasible 41

    How to Improve Your Rehearsals 42

Saving the Fundamental Tracks 45

    The Tracking Session 45

Overdubbing 49

    The Process 49

    An Important Note About Vocals 51

    The Emotional Aspect 52

    How to Record a Song in Five Easy Steps 53

    How to Record Vocals 54

    The Proper Microphone Techniques 56

    How to Record Musical Instruments 57

Editing the Music 67
   What Does "Music Editing" Mean? 67
   The Process 67
Mixing the Music 71
   The Basic Music Mixing Procedure 71
Mastering the Recording 77
   The Process of Mastering Songs 77
Conclusion 81
Other Related Books 83
Photo Credits 85

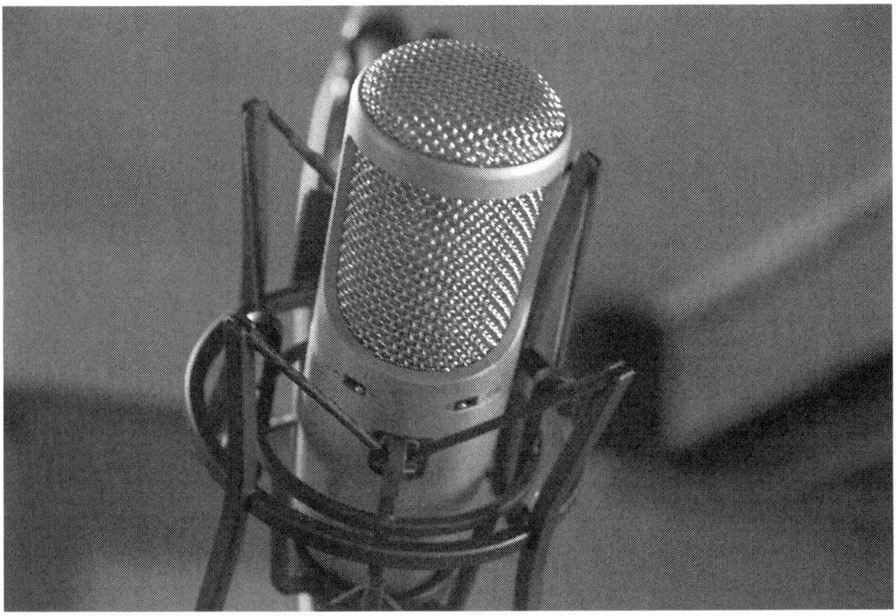

Introduction

Thank you for purchasing, " Home Recording 101".

This book contains various steps and strategies on how to set up your very own home recording studio even though you only have a limited budget.

Inside you will find chapters that will introduce you to the most critical hardware and software that you should acquire for your recording booth. You will also discover several cost-efficient tips that will help you in designing your studio.

This book is ideal for beginners who want to learn the basics of music recording.

Thanks again for downloading this book, I hope you enjoy it!

Rake

Essential Hardware

In order to record and produce the best music, you need to have good hardware, and in this day and age you need good software, too!

If you are just starting your home recording studio, you may not have adequate funds to buy the best audio equipment on the market. However, that does not mean that cheap items always produce bad quality. As a beginner, you don't really need a lot of fancy pieces of audio equipment.

If you have the essential tools, it will be easier for you to start your career as a music producer. And if you work hard on your craft and you want to reach a more professional level, you can start investing more in advanced audio recording hardware. To get you started, here are some of the essential tools that you should have in your home recording studio.

Microphone

The microphone is considered one of the most important elements in your indoor studio. When you are shopping for equipment on a limited budget, the best option that you can pick is a $100 microphone. Even though it is not too expensive, it can help you record vocals and sounds clearly.

But if you really want to buy something cheaper, you can go for a mini microphone that can be plugged into a USB port. This one costs less than $80 a piece. However, this type of product is more effective for recording podcasts rather than music. In addition, the things that you can do with this microphone are very limited.

Once you have obtained enough money, you can invest in a condenser microphone that uses a cardioid pickup audio outline. With this tool, you can easily record audio with a fuller and crystal-clear quality.

Audio Interface

This recording equipment connects your microphone or musical instrument to a nearby computer. You can also use this to link the studio monitors together. Unfortunately, you need to shell out a few bucks on this tool. An audio interface that is extremely cheap is not a good investment because it has limited features. Also, it might negatively affect your audio recording process.

If you are a beginner, you can buy audio interfaces from manufacturers such as Apogee or Focusrite. They produce well-designed recording equipment that is not too pricey. A $200 audio interface from these companies can be a great addition to your budding home recording studio.

But if you want to save up, you can also buy a secondhand Apogee and Focusrite equipment online. Obviously, just make sure that the previous owner is very responsible, and the equipment that he sells isn't damaged.

Digital Keyboard

Digital keyboards are advantageous if you are recording a set of live music. The main purpose of this tool is to play synthesized or sampled musical instruments. Most music producers also use this to enhance their music and add some computer-generated audio effects. The standard number of keys on a piano should be 88. But most digital keyboards, especially those that cost $100, only have 49. Unless you are producing classical music, this will not be much of a problem to you. There are even some handy digital keyboards that only have 32 keys. They may have limited features, but you can still use them for playing basic sounds. And if you are traveling somewhere far to play your tunes, it will be easier for you to bring this miniature keyboard during your trips.

Studio Monitors

Basically, studio monitors are just speakers. However, they are a little bit different than the ones that you usually plug into your computers or iPods. Usually, most of these speakers can only be plugged into a computer using a single cable. In addition, you also need to purchase another stereo cable just to plug it in your other mobile devices. They can produce a colored sound. This means that some of the audio signals are emphasized. These computer speakers will either produce a heavy bass or a sharp pitch that does not have any mid-range. In a nutshell, you will not hear clear audio if you use a basic computer speaker.

They will work fine if you are just watching movies, or playing games. However, you cannot use this for mixing beats because the sound that you will hear is not totally accurate.

Although no studio monitor can ever produce a 100% uncolored sound, it is still recommended audio equipment because it can create acoustics that are extremely close to reality.

Since they are vital components in the audio mixing process, you need to prioritize the quality of your studio monitors. So as much as possible, buy equipment that is brand new. The cheapest studio monitors that you can buy are probably around $300. The price may be a little bit high, but you can ensure that the quality is top notch. I prefer KRK Rokit monitors (pictured above)

Headphones

Now that you have studio monitors, do you still need a pair of headphones to listen to your tracks? Apparently, yes. Headphones are not just accessories to make you look like a cool DJ. Music producers use this for referencing. This is a process for inspecting how your beats will sound like in devices that are not geared for audio mixing. Since most of your audience will not listen to your music via studio monitors, it is important that you also check the sound quality from the consumer's perspective. $100 is about the normal price for buying a good pair of headphones. You do not need to buy cans that cost more than $300 because you will do most of the audio production using your studio monitors anyway.

Cables

The most vital cables that you will need are XLR cables for the microphone, and a couple of ¼ inch TS cables for the musical instruments or studio monitors. These are extremely cheap items, so it is best that you buy a lot of them. You will never know when you need a spare cable.

Computer

If you don't have a complete mixing board available, you can purchase a computer and set up your digital audio workstation (DAW). Most computer programs can already provide you with a customizable DAW that is replete with all the tools that you need for audio editing and mixing. Since you do not need to have to deal with 3D and video editing, you do not need a device with powerful specs. You only need the following:

- 4 GB RAM
- Dual Core or Core i3 GPU
- Sound card
- Video card
- 1 TB internal memory

Essential Software

Aside from the hardware, another vital component in your home recording studio is the audio editing and mixing programs. With these pieces of software, you can remove noise from your tracks, convert your audio files in the right format, and add some cool effects that come to your mind.

There is a lot of editing software that is available on the online market. Some even offer free installations. However, you should be very careful about choosing your programs because not all of them offer stellar features. This chapter lists the best and most reliable audio editing software that you should get for your home recording studio.

Audacity

Because of its simplicity, Audacity is some of the best audio editing software for fledgling sound producers. Even though it is not a digital audio workstation, it still has a lot of nifty features up its sleeve. With audacity, you can polish your tracks before posting them your website, normalize the sound levels, and remove any noise in your audio.

This is a program that is very easy to master. Audacity can support numerous file types such as WAV, mp3, and others. You can also use this software for recording your live audio. It is also an excellent tool for creating basement mixes and turning converting vinyl songs into digital format. Lastly, Audacity is totally free to download.

Adobe Audition

Audition is a slightly powerful program that can splice, restore, and remix audio in a hassle-free way. It is pretty expensive if you purchase it on its own. However, you will may get a discount if you buy it in its Creative Suite version.

It has a very user-friendly interface so you will not have any problems in working with this software. However, a little knowledge about Adobe's digital workstation can significantly help you to process your work faster.

This software is also replete with its own array of sound effects. You can use them to add a lot of flair to your tracks.

Reaper

Reaper is a digital audio workstation that offers flexibility, a vast array of features and a lot of customizable options. To make your experience better, you can even install a lot of plug-ins. Even though you are new to audio recording, you will enjoy playing around with this software because its user interface is pretty easy to master.

Another advantage of using Reaper is that it can work well even if your recording hardware is not that powerful. You can edit all your tracks using its library of special effects. At the time of this writing, you can purchase Reaper for $60. If you have some money to spare, you can buy the professional version at around $225.

Ableton Live

This software is a very nifty digital audio workstation that produces sounds and edits your audio files at the same time. Most music enthusiasts enjoy using Ableton Live because it is replete with a lot of professional tools. A lot of its features are geared more towards live sound recordings. However, that does not mean that it is useless when you produce your own music.

Ableton Live is highly recommended for advanced users because of its vast collection of features and effects. In addition, its interface is more complex than the average software.

Mix Vibes

This easy-to-use software can support 16 different tracks at the same time. In addition, it can also support different audio file formats. It has an equalizer, sound effects library, and other nifty tools that you usually need for your audio recording tasks. Mix Vibes is free to download, and it works on Windows operating system.

Loop Labs

Loop Labs is another professional audio mixing program that comes with presets on multiple channels, remixing tools, and MP3 sampling. It can accommodate 32 individual channels at a time which makes your audio editing experience easier and faster. In addition, you can also compose your own tracks with Loop Labs.

Tactile

Tactile acts as a powerhouse audio mixing software. It has several turntables, as well as a couple of nifty controls for changing the speed of your audio, editing frequencies, and remixing the audio levels of each individual song on your playlist. You can get this program for free, and it works on Windows operating system.

And so many more. I personally prefer Sonar (X Series, pictured above) by Cakewalk. It's the one I learned on, and I find that it has everything that I need and more. Pro Tools is also a very popular software used by studios small and large.

Designing the Home Recording Studio

Before you buy any large equipment for your home studio, you first need to focus your attention and resources on constructing your recording room. Keep in mind that it is easier to upgrade your audio hardware than it is to change one of the rooms to make it more sound-proof.

For most people, a recording studio is only perceived as a large room that has carpeted walls, foamed ceilings, piles of CD's, and a bass trap. Unfortunately, it's not as simple as that. To create a well-built home recording studio, you need to do a lot hard work and research. If you construct your room using the wrong materials, you will not be able to produce or record your music accurately.

When building your home studio, you'll need to adjust the dimensions of your room to accommodate the double walls, additional ceilings, or floating floors that you will place there. If you place your recording room on the upper floors of your house, you need to make sure that your ground floor can support all of the extra weight that will come from the upper room. This means that you might have to make some renovations in your home.

However, you do not need to worry too much about the budget. Constructing a recording studio is more about using the right design theories and less about using the most expensive materials on the market. This chapter will discuss effective tips and strategies for designing your home studio without going over the budget.

Sound Isolation

The idea here is to create a room that will eliminate or reduce the sound levels from any source. Sound isolation deals with removing any unwanted noise while you are recording. This includes preventing the whirring of your neighbor's lawnmower or the loud beep of a car horn from penetrating your studio.

Also, sound isolation is also used if you want to segregate each recorded sound in your tracks. For instance, you need to reduce the decibel levels of a drum kit to prevent the sound of a snare drum from blending in your vocal tracks during a multi-track recording session.

You can easily create a recording room with efficient sound isolating capabilities even if you do not spend a lot of money. However, you need to carefully consider the space of your studio and the sources of your sound.

Are you editing your tracks in your basement? Are there any other rooms on top of your studio? Where are your windows located? Search for areas in your home where outside noise can be easily isolated.

You should focus on isolating the sound from percussion or acoustic drum kits because they produce the highest decibel levels among other musical instruments. These pieces of equipment should have a separated mini booth that is made from walls that can segregate sound. You can build one by using a material that has high-density levels. Examples of this one are high walls, insulation, and interior studs. The array of interior studs is vital in building a sturdy barrier that can deflect any unwanted vibrations.

To add more density to your ceiling and prevent any noise from bleeding outside of the other rooms, you can opt to line it with an R-19 installation. You should also add drywall because it is denser and cheaper.

Sound Absorption

This concept, on the other hand, is more about controlling the decay of your audio sources so that they will not create a lot of unnecessary echo inside your recording studio. Usually, large rooms with smooth walls need to be altered thoroughly so that they can absorb sound better. .

If you only enclose your recording studio with drywall, you will notice that the audio that you will produce is quite different. It feels like you are recording from a shower room. That is because sound waves with extremely high frequencies tend to bounce off in smoother surfaces. To reduce the echo in your recording studio, there are cost-efficient ways to fix it.

For cement and wooden floors with smooth surfaces, you can opt to cover them with throw rugs or cheap carpets. A thicker drywall and some sheet rocks can "roughen" your wall and ceiling so that they can absorb the sound better.

Use egg crate foams

Professional-grade studio panels that are made from fine foam can be very expensive. If you are just starting your career, you can substitute this material with egg crate foams and bed liners from foam mattresses. Just attach them to your wall using a staple wire and a glue gun. You will be amazed at how clear your audio will be once you set these items up.

Use acoustic traps

Absorbing sound from acoustic instruments that produce lower frequency levels can be a daunting task. However, you can easily do this by setting up acoustic traps. These tools can also reduce the reverb time in the recording studio, as well as produce "drier" sounds.

You should use acoustic traps instead of duvet covers because the latter is only effective in absorbing sound that has high-frequency levels. You can place these traps on your walls or windows.

Do not place parallel walls

Parallel walls only create standing waves – a condition in which the frequency levels are inconsistent in several areas of your recording studio. To prevent standing waves from occurring, you can apply damping materials and traps at certain angles on your wall.

Allow light to enter your studio

Daylight is an important component in building a pleasant working environment. Lack of sunshine in your studio will make you feel like you are locked in a prison camp. Most people usually board up their windows just to prevent sound from leaking outside of their rooms. However, two sheets of acoustic glass and double glazed windows that do not have any openings will work wonders for your studio, as long as you install them correctly.

Seal your doors

Similar to your windows, the doorway is another problematic area where sound usually leaks out. You need to install a heavy door to ensure that noise will not come in your recording studio. Also, you should also apply a sheet block to further isolate your sounds.

Do not forget to install proper ventilation

Most music producers get so excited with installing sound barriers that they forget one important thing – how to breathe properly inside the recording booth. Make sure that you provide an inlet and an outlet inside your room. They should be properly separated, and one of them should have a fan.

In designing and building your home recording studio, you should remember that it is a very time-consuming process. You cannot really expect that you can build one in just a single day, especially if you do not have enough financial resources. There are also instances wherein you will encounter some setbacks while working on it. The entire process can be quite frustrating and complicated. However, it is important that you do not quit. Once you have finally finished your studio, this space will be yours to use and enjoy.

Recording Tips for Various Musical Instruments

How do you usually record the sound from your guitars and drums?

There are many factors that you need to consider if you want to properly capture the sound of musical instruments. You have to think about where you should place the microphone and how to tune your guitars properly so that the sound that you will get is clear and lush. Here are some useful tips on doing that properly.

How to Tune your Instruments

Before you start recording, you have to make sure that you have properly tuned your instruments first. Tuning may just be a little thing in the whole music production process, but it can make an enormous impact on the overall quality of your tracks.

Tuning your Drum Kit

This process is often overlooked by musicians, especially those who are quite new to the recording industry. That is because most drummers who play during live sessions are not very knowledgeable about the different sounds that their drum kit produces. It is also harder to distinguish the sound of percussion instruments during live performances, especially if you are playing in a band.

A drum kit that is out of tune can easily be heard in a recording studio because that room is built to absorb and isolate sound.

There are a lot of theories when it comes to tuning the drum kit during a recording session. Some prefer to tune it based on the track that will be played. Other people, on the other hand, base their decision on the instrument's resonant frequency.

The first thing that you have to do is to tune your snare drums because they are the most prominent percussion instruments in the set. A lot of drummers play different types of snare drums during a recording session. You have to make sure that your snare drums do not rattle or resonate too much.

To prevent that from happening, check the position of the instrument. Is it too straight and rigid? Try to loosen up its lower head to reduce the buzzing sound from your snare wires.

If your drum kit is producing too much resonant vibration, it is probably caused by your toms. Hit each tom to see who is causing the most buzz. Re-tune the instrument that causes the problem. Or, you can use a muffling ring.

Lastly, the upper and lower heads of your tom drum should each have a different pitch to lessen its resonance. The top portion's pitch should be slightly higher than the bottom.

Tuning your kick drum can also be a daunting task. If you make it sound too low, it will not have enough punch.

But if you tune it too high, it will negatively affect the instrument's thump. To solve this dilemma, you have to make sure that your microphone is placed in the right position whenever you record this instrument. You can place it a little bit near or slightly far away from the instrument. This decision will depend on the type of track that you are playing.

Tuning your String Instruments

Searching for the right pitch of your stringed instruments can be a pretty daunting task. That is because you can't really tune a fretted instrument such as a guitar or bass using a chromatic scale with twelve tones. The best thing that you can do is to alter the intonation of your instrument so that the octaves, fifths, and other prominent intervals will be properly heard during the recording session.

To do this, you need the help of a tuner. Even though you can tune your instrument by just using your ears, you still need this device in more to make the right changes. There are several different types of tuners that are available on the market. But if you do not want to buy one, you can just download a tuning app on your mobile devices. They are accurate and handier than the ones that are sold in music shops. Most of these apps are also free to use.

When tuning your guitar, make sure that you shut off all of the effects like the EQ and reverb because they can affect the readings of your tuner. Choose the rhythm pickup of the instrument rather than its bridge pickup. Pluck the strings lightly because doing otherwise will produce an inaccurate sound.

Basic Recording Tips – Percussion

1. **Place the instrument directly on your microphone** – This is effective for smaller percussion instruments that produce a lower sound level. If you place your microphone in front of your instrument, you will be able to capture a fuller sound, and its subtle tunes will be more emphasized.

2. **Across the microphone** – But if you do not want to emphasize the sound of your percussion, position the microphone across it. This method will flatten out the sound.

3. **Use two microphones at the same time** – This is known as the Blumlein array. This method works on a more dynamic percussion instrument because it provides realism. It also provides extra dimensions that no single microphone can ever do.

4. **Record room ambiance** – Place a condenser microphone with a cardioid tube at least four and a half feet from your percussion instrument. This will help your recorded sounds become more balanced and refined.

Basic Recording Tips – Acoustic Guitar

1. **Use a ribbon microphone** – using a pair of ribbon microphones and arranging them in a Blumlein array will help you capture a more natural acoustic guitar sound. It will be easier for you to record all of the warmth and detail

that you need to create fuller beats. Also, it can also handle a lot of EQ.

2. **Adjust the position of your microphones from time to time** – If your guitar is pretty close to the microphone, you can capture a warmer sound. So if you notice the recorded track is too warm, you should adjust the distance between your instrument and microphone. Ideally, the ribbon microphone works best if you place it three of four inches away from your acoustic guitar.

3. **Place your mono microphone on the right fret** – The best position of your mono microphone should be 6 to 8 inches away from the 12th fret of your guitar.

4. **Apply the Blumlein array** – This method can also be used on acoustic guitars too. Make sure that the pair of microphones is placed 90 degrees apart. One microphone should be facing the body of your instrument while the other one is facing its neck. To record a fuller sound, use the back of the microphones.

How to Record Music

Now that you have created your own recording studio, it is time to discuss the process of recording music. In general, music recording has confused millions of inexperienced artists, songwriters, and sound engineers all over the world. Since these beginners do not know how the pros produce music, they are forced to implement a trial-and-error strategy.

This chapter will discuss the basics of music production. It will provide you with the basic concepts and methods that you can use in recording your own music. Here we go:

The Basics

Music experts divide the production process into eight steps. This segmentation is done to simplify the procedure. These steps are:

1. Writing the song
2. Saving a Demo Copy
3. Rehearsals
4. Saving the Fundamental Tracks
5. Overdubbing
6. Music Editing
7. Mixing
8. Mastering

Each step serves an important role in the process of music recording. Combining or skipping steps is not advisable since it often leads to poor results. Unfortunately, many people try to skip or combine some of these steps to save money. These people do not know that by doing so, they are turning a simple and easy process into a complicated one.

The "It Will Be Fixed During the Mix" Strategy

Many music producers work on their projects too quickly. They rush the process and simply record the tracks. In general, these people think that they can just improve the quality of the songs during the "mixing" stage. However, this kind of strategy is doomed to fail. You won't be able to create great music if you ignore the problems that will appear during the early stages of the process. These problems often "snowball" (i.e. they pile up at a blinding speed), which may turn your project into a useless enterprise.

Delaying the process of correcting errors is a bad idea. In general, you will need several hours to feel the subtleties of the piece, get into the right mindset, and make the proper judgments about how to correct the errors. You should always try to fix the problems as soon as you notice them. Often, these problems can be solved by spending a few minutes on a retake or completing the necessary tasks before moving on to the next step.

The Eight Steps of the Process

The next chapters will discuss each step in detail. Study these chapters carefully since they can help you become a successful music producer. Here, you will learn how the entire recording process works: from songwriting to CD mastering.

Writing the Song

This step may start with a melody, a distinct sound, a chord progression, or an improvisation that deserves a title and some lyrics. Once you have chosen the topic of your song, you may begin the songwriting process. This chapter will discuss two types of songwriting techniques: traditional and modern.

The Traditional Technique

This technique requires you to write a song using a melody played on a single instrument. According to music experts, this is the reason that lots of songs were created as a "guitar-and-vocal piece" or a "piano-and-vocal" piece. If you are working with other musicians, they might become bored if you will waste time trying out various lyrics and melodies. It would be best if you will finalize these aspects of your song alone. Work with other people only when you are fully satisfied with the lyric and melodic aspects of the song.

The Modern Technique

This songwriting technique involves the use of new technology. Nowadays, you don't need to have a band when recording songs. You may produce song templates that can help you work on your projects without having to perform music passages repeatedly. In general, the modern technique utilizes sound samples and music loops to trigger the songwriter's creativity.

This technique also has its own share of drawbacks. The most obvious drawback is that the writer might concentrate on the production aspects rather than the songwriting itself. Many songwriters have failed to notice weak lyrics and melodies because they got distracted with the technology they were using. This situation often results in wasted time and resources.

The Four Fundamental Principles of Songwriting

To help you understand this step better, this section will explain the songwriting principles and how they influence the entire music recording process.

1. The Song's Subject Matter – Before you start writing, you have to answer these two questions:

    —What is this song about?

    —Which feelings are you trying to convey?

    The answer to these questions will serve as the foundation for all the decisions that you will make regarding this project. In general, the subject matter of your song will help you determine the effects and instruments that need to be used. For example, when writing about drug addiction, you should not use tinkling bells in recording the song later. The selected theme is serious, so employing upbeat sounds (e.g. bells) may not be a good idea unless you are trying to make a statement.

2. The Song's Story – How will you convey your song's message? You may use simple techniques such as using the minor scales when writing sad songs. Also, you have to make sure that the song's lyrics and melody are supporting each other. You should consider the message of your lyrics when choosing keys and chords.

3. Hold the Listener's Attention – How are you going to present the musical piece? Do you want the song to start calmly and end with a bang? Do you like it to begin with big sounds, calm down a bit and then erupt in the end? Do you want your song to have a consistent level of energy all throughout? While answering these questions, you also need to consider the message of your song.

The classic song pattern begins with a verse that tells about a situation. It tells the listener what happened, how the singer/writer got into that situation. The chorus part then expresses the feelings that came from the situation that has been shared. Thus, the chorus tells the audience what had happened because of the situation told during the song's verse.

Often, back and forth progressions are present between the song's verse and chorus parts. These repetitive progressions might lead into a bridge or breakdown section. The bridge/breakdown part of the song gives more information about the story. Sometimes, it gives the listener a new point of view regarding the situation being shared.

The traditional structure outlined above is not required if you have your own way of keeping your listeners interested. You have to consider the message of your song when choosing a structure. Songs that focus on the redundancy of working and living in a huge city will benefit from repetitive sound loops or programmed rhythms. The repetitive and computerized nature of the music can help in conveying the feeling of having a robotic lifestyle.

The main reason the classic structure (that is, the verse-chorus-bridge method) works is effective is that it is a template that possesses an excellent chance of keeping the listeners' attention. Each story involves a setup (i.e. the verse), a problem or effect (i.e. the chorus), a solution or realization (i.e. the bridge), and an ending.

4. Feelings Over Thoughts – Well-written songs indicate the type of sound dynamics that must be used. The musical piece itself can help you decide whether a bridge section is needed or

not. It will tell you the perfect techniques to use in each of its parts. For example, the song may require you to use simple melodies or complex instrumentals.

Saving a Demo Copy

Once you are satisfied with the song you wrote, it's time to record a demo version of that project. This demo can be simple or grand. For example, you may sing the song while playing a single instrument (e.g. piano or guitar) or involve a whole set of musical instruments (including a drum set). The choice is up to you. During this stage, you should focus on expressing the core message of your composition. This will serve as a reference for everyone who will be working on that song.

The Importance of the Demo Stage

This part of the music production process can help you in many ways. For instance, it can help you polish transitions, improve the lyrics, identify problematic song sections, etc. This stage also allows you to gather more ideas about the project. While recording a demo copy, you may discover new concepts that can improve the song you are working on.

Professional music producers refer to this step as an "idea generator." It allows them to know the things that must be included in the song before starting the actual process of recording the final product. It is a huge waste of time and resources to complete all the stages of song recording just to find out that the output has an undesirable quality.

Thus, the demo stage can help you make sure that your song will have excellent quality.

The Process of Recording a Demo

The latest technological advancements have significantly simplified the tasks of a music producer. Nowadays, you may use almost any type of musical instrument to improve your composition. You have a broad range of options: from recorded sounds and digital loops to raw audio libraries that require you to interact with the sound you are interested in. Regardless of your chosen music genre, you will find an audio library that can help fulfill your visions regarding your song.

Two Factors You Need to Consider

1. Honesty – When working on your own song, it is sometimes difficult to be honest with yourself regarding the best and worst parts of the musical piece. It is not easy to criticize the project since you were the one who created it. In general, songwriters tend to become biased regarding their own work.

    People naturally memorize lyrics and melodies after hearing a musical piece several times. This situation causes the individuals who are working on the song to think that the project is already in its best form. They cannot analyze the project objectively since they don't have the point-of-view of an individual who hears the song for the first time.

This problem can be solved by having a recording partner. Make sure that your partner won't hear the piece during the songwriting stage.

2. Feedback – People who are sensitive to honest opinions lose great opportunities to improve their projects. As a general rule, you should keep an open mind while working on songs. Remember that the feedback given by other people is not always correct. Use the opinion of others as a guide in detecting the flaws in your project. Don't worry about their suggestions: you will still make the final decisions regarding your work.

The Rehearsals

The rehearsal stage plays an important role in ensuring the quality of a recorded song. Unfortunately, music artists tend to ignore it. People often associate rehearsals with live/actual performances. They don't know that rehearsals are also necessary when preparing for recording sessions.

In general, this stage helps you to make sure that the performer knows what to do and how to do it. It is not unusual for artists to waste several hours inside a recording studio just to get a great take. They work on the vocals, instrumentals, and song arrangement during a time that was supposed to be used for the actual song recording. Thus, you will be able to save your time and resources just by spending enough time on the rehearsal phase. You can detect and fix problems more quickly during the rehearsal stage compared to the recording stage.

This chapter will discuss the things you have to consider when rehearsing for your songs. It will also explain the important aspects of working with your bandmates (if you are in a band).

The Benefits of Conducting Band Rehearsals

1. The performers will know the song's arrangement.
2. They will know the ideal tempo for the song.
3. They will understand the song's individual parts and how those parts work together.
4. The band members will know the ideal tone, sound, and instrument for each part of the song.
5. They will find and solve problems that were not detected during the demo stage.
6. The members of the band will have the chance to share their own ideas. These ideas can help in improving the song's quality.
7. It allows you to remove performers who don't have the proper feel or skills for the song.
8. It helps you to identify the additional resources you might need for the recording stage.
9. It allows you to create a reference copy that you can use for the recording phase.

You should rehearse before recording your songs, regardless of your chosen music genre. Also, remember that studio recordings are completely different from stage performances. When listening to an audio recording, people won't see you singing or playing an instrument. That means you should convey your passion through the music you record.

How Rehearsals Influence the Recording Stage

The recording studio presents an unnatural working environment. Here, musicians have to use headphones and isolation booths. This limited hearing and vision might affect the musician's overall performance. For instance, bass players who use a direct box cannot feel the vibrations produced by the amplifier. The absence of sight lines between the band members will also eliminate the subtle visual cues used by musicians to improve their performance.

Because of the reasons explained above, all of the performers should be well rehearsed prior to entering the studio. If they didn't have enough practice, minor issues such as limited vision might cause frustration and/or confusion. At times, even minor headphone problems may destroy a band's performance.

How to Organize Band Rehearsals

Obviously, you can organize a band rehearsal just by employing a "get all the members there" strategy. However, you can boost your band's productivity and efficiency by planning certain aspects of the rehearsal. Here are some techniques used by professional music recorders:

1. *<u>Send the demonstration copies of the song to all the band members</u>* – This is an easy task. Save the demo copy as an .mp3 file and send it as an email attachment. Alternatively, you may share the file using an online collaboration tool such as box.com and dropbox.com. This will help you ensure

that all of the performers are familiar with the song. However, this may be unnecessary if your bandmates have helped you in the songwriting phase.

2. *Schedule the Rehearsals* – Make sure that only the needed band members are present in the rehearsal studio. For instance, it would be not necessary to have the presence of your saxophone player if your song doesn't involve that particular instrument.

    According to music experts, you should use a "bottom up" strategy when rehearsing your songs. That means you will rehearse the song by working on its individual parts one by one. For example, you may focus on the rhythm section first. Analyzing the quality of that section will be easy and simple since the sound will not be muddled by other sections (e.g. vocals, bass guitar, lead guitar, etc.). Once all of the issues have been corrected, you may move to the next section of the song.

Rehearsal for the Vocalist

Rehearsals help vocalists to become prepared for the upcoming studio recordings. During rehearsals, the vocalist must focus on the technical elements of the performance (e.g. pitch, phrasing, timing, etc.). If the vocalist encounters problems such as unreachable notes or tongue twisters, he/she can work with the songwriter to improve the song's quality.

Once all of the technical issues have been solved, a "raw" vocal needs to be recorded immediately. This recording will serve as a reference for the later stages of the recording process. If the performers have rehearsed well, the music producer may concentrate on the important elements such as the emotion, message, and flow of the song. These elements are crucial since they influence listeners to purchase songs.

The Things You Can Do If Rehearsals Are Not Feasible

Nowadays, tasks must be completed without spending too much time or money. This is the reason why rehearsals cannot be done sometimes. If time and budget constraints are affecting your options, you can solve your problems by using your creativity and resourcefulness. Here are some tricks that you can use:

1. Send demo copies, chord charts, and music scores using the internet.
2. Set up video conferences with the performers. If this is not possible, you may work with the rest of your team using ordinary phone calls.

You should use the tricks given above to prepare your bandmates for the recording process. Since you have sent the information they need, they can generate ideas and practice their parts whenever they want. It would be great if you will ask your bandmates to record and share their rehearsals with you. This way, you will have a chance to know what your bandmates have to offer and, integrate their input into the recording process.

How to Improve Your Rehearsals

Rehearsals are important in the recording process because they help the musicians prepare for their roles. Here are some tips that can help you boost the productivity and effectiveness of your rehearsals.

- Do not "over-rehearse" a musical piece – If the performers are getting bored or frustrated with a particular song, work on a different one that can be played easily. This trick will help you to refresh everyone, allowing you to work on the difficult song again later.

  If a certain member is having difficulties with his part, you may simplify it or tell him to polish it on his own before the next band practice. This will reduce or eliminate the frustration of other members who might make the problem worse.

- Use a recorded song for the vocalist's rehearsals – You should record a good rhythm section from the band members. That recording can help you in rehearsing the band's vocalist. With this strategy, you won't have to force the rest of the band to play the same part repeatedly. You may bring all the members together for a last band rehearsal prior to the actual recording.

- Perform the song in front of other people – If you think that the performers are getting bored, you should schedule a live show before recording the song. This trick will help you to inject some life into the recording. In general, performers love the feeling of being on stage. Performing in front of a live audience will allow your bandmates to apply the skills they have worked on persistently. After this live performance, your band will be 100% ready to get inside your recording studio.

Saving the Fundamental Tracks

Establishing the fundamental track is like repeating the entire process using a more sensitive ear. During this phase, you will analyze the different aspects of your song (e.g. pitch, timing, dynamics, tone, etc.) critically. In general, fundamental tracks (also called basic tracks) are used as the foundation of a musical piece. The performers focus on the rhythm parts, particularly the bass and drums.

This chapter will provide you with tips and techniques that you can use in your home studio.

The Tracking Session

Obviously, recording the basic tracks inside a home studio is harder than doing it in a professional studio. Here are the things you need to consider:

1. Position the instruments carefully:
    a. Drums—If you are working in a small studio, you should find the best location for your drums using the kick drum. In small areas, this drum is greatly affected by resonances produced by the room. You have to move the kick drum so that it faces the center of the studio. Place it in a spacious area: make sure that there

is enough space for the drummer and the rest of the drum set.

    b.   Guitar and Bass Amplifiers – Place these pieces of equipment on a table to reduce resonance created by the floor. Amplifiers that produce thin sounds must be placed near a wall. The wall will reflect the sound waves, adding more frequencies to the music.

2. Use Gobos – A gobo (abbreviation for "go between") is a movable barrier positioned between instruments. This barrier can absorb or reflect sound waves produced during a performance. In general, you should use gobos to control or tighten the reverbs created by the room. Reverbs may affect the song you are recording, particularly the sounds processed by the close microphones.

You have to place a semicircular wall of gobos around the drums. This trick will minimize the reverbs that may add unwanted color or flatness to the drums' sounds.

3. Microphone Techniques – There are different kinds of microphones that you can use in recording the basic tracks. For professional musicians, the most important microphones for a drum set are the overhead, snare, and kick microphones. The overhead mic captures the essence of the sounds created by the drums. Thus, it plays a huge role in the

track recording phase. It catches the sounds produced by the snare, kick, and cymbals.

In general, you will experience difficulties in getting a good basic track if you are working with many microphones. Limit the number of microphones inside your home recording studio.

4. Setting the Sound Levels – Make sure that there is enough "headroom" (i.e. the level by which the audio-handling abilities of a sound system can exceed an assigned point) when working on your song's basic tracks. Keep in mind that the sounds in the recorded song are louder than those produced inside the recording studio. When recording songs, you should set your sound levels about four to six "dbFS" (decibels to full scale) lower than your desired sound volume.

You shouldn't set sounds for a song unless the performers are playing the right part at the right tempo. This is perhaps the most common mistake committed by beginners when working on basic tracks. For instance, if a guitarist is playing at 140 bpm (beats per minute), but the musical piece you are working on is at 120 bpm, you will be choking up the sound excessively that the guitar sound cannot resonate correctly. If the performer has a lower bpm than the song, however, the sounds will be loose and open. These sounds become "murky" and indistinct when played at a faster tempo.

Remember that no one sound will work for all of your songs. You have to make modifications for every track. In general, you must record songs that have the same vibe and tempo. With this strategy, you can minimize the required adjustments. You should compensate for the song's tempo by adjusting the acoustics inside the drum room. Songs with a fast tempo need a drum room that has "dead" acoustics. Conversely, slow songs require a drum room that can produce lots of reverb. You can deaden the acoustics of a room using rugs, pillows, blankets, and mattresses.

5. Headphones and Communication – There are two things that can mess up an excellent recording setup: (1) bad headphones and (2) lack of communication. In general, you need to make sure that your headphone mix works for all of the performers. This is an important aspect when recording a song's basic tracks.

It's a good idea to place talkback microphones in your home studio to allow communication during breaks. You don't have to connect these microphones onto a recorder. Some music producers run these microphones through a little mixer so they can be linked to the headphone mixes being used.

Overdubbing

Overdubbing (also called sweetening) is the procedure that allows you to record performances and a pre-recorded audio file synchronously. It's like each instrument used for the song will have its own track. Since each performer is acoustically isolated from the others, you may rerecord whenever you want without affecting the rest of the group.

In general, overdubbing is difficult to master. Since the performer won't have visual cues that can lead him through the song, he is required to record his part blindly against the pre-recorded material. Visual cues help musicians by showing the subtle pulls and pushes of a song. Thus, the overdubbing musician is required to guess or adjust his performance so that it matches the recorded track.

The Process

Since the overdubbing stage is inherently difficult, you have to make sure that all performers are well-prepared. Although preparations don't guarantee that everything will be perfect, they allow you to adjust quickly whenever unexpected events occur.

It is common for performers to overestimate what they can do on any given recording session. Regardless of how you plan your recording sessions, there will be things that you just can't control. If your vocalist arrives with a cold, you might have lots of extra time. Here are some things that can help you in your overdubbing sessions:

1. Establish what you are trying to accomplish.
2. Make sure that you have all the resources you need.
3. Make sure that every part has been rehearsed and that every performance-related issue has been solved.
4. The musicians must play their parts at the correct tempo.
5. Make sure that there is enough space in your recording studio. This will help the performers to feel comfortable with what they are doing.
6. Make sure that you have a second plan, in case something goes wrong with your first one.
7. You shouldn't rush through the recordings just to attain your goals for that session.
8. Don't settle for mediocre performances that require lots of editing.
9. Once you capture the essence of a section, record it immediately.
10. Take breaks on a regular basis. This is important, especially if there is confusion and frustration in the recording studio.
11. You should communicate with the musicians after each take. Give them tips on how to improve their performance.

An Important Note About Vocals

Recording the vocals is probably the most difficult aspect of the overdubbing stage. The vocalist often feels tremendous pressure since his performance is considered as the core of the entire song. Depending on the artist's personality, the overdubbing stage can be a walk in the park or a hellish nightmare. Some vocalists like to overcome difficulties, some collapse under them. The way you will manage these scenarios will make or break your recording session.

According to music experts, the process of recording vocals has two aspects: technical and emotional. The technical aspect is easy to polish though artists may overlook certain details that can affect the performance negatively. Here are some tips that can help you with the technical aspect:

- Make sure that the vocalist feels comfortable inside the recording studio.
- Make sure that unnecessary things (e.g. unused cables) are out of the way.
- Give the vocalist everything he needs.
- Make sure that the microphone is positioned correctly. It must not hinder the vocalist's view of the lyric sheet.
- Use a pop screen to mark a comfortable distance between the microphone and the performer.
- Make sure that you have an excellent headphone mix. The vocalist must hear his voice clearly. He or she must feel the energy coming from the music.

- Talk to the vocalist after each take. You should never leave him inside the recording room guessing what will happen next.

The Emotional Aspect

It is hard to predict what the vocalist's emotions will be when he enters the recording room. Some people panic, convulse, and even vomit when they set foot in that mysterious place called recording studio. Others, however, are ready to give the performance of their life. In general, individuals show their real personality when they are under pressure. This is the reason you should establish trust with your musicians prior to recording the song.

If you are planning to record and produce songs to make money, you need to learn some things about human psychology. You are going to work with other human beings so it would be great if you will know how humans think. This way, you will be able to motivate your artists so they can give top-notch performances. Remember that the vocalist plays a huge part in your recordings. Make sure that he is comfortable in the studio: this will help him to express the right emotions. Here are some tips that can help you with the emotional aspect:

- Set up a comfortable recording studio.
- Talk to the vocalist before doing the recording. Discuss the song and tell him the emotions needed for that session.
- Don't overwork your vocalist. If he isn't getting the right emotions, take a break or work on something

else. This will help you to refocus the vocalist's energy.
- Allow your vocalist to express his frustrations. Often, a frustrated artist will have problems in giving his best performance.
- Respect your vocalist.
- Don't focus on the technical problems (e.g. pitch, timing, etc.). These issues are often caused by overexertion or the inability to feel the song through a headphone.
- Remember that performance is more important than sound quality.

How to Record a Song in Five Easy Steps

1. Record the Basic Tracks – This has been discussed in the previous chapter.

2. Record the Song's Rhythm Section – The rhythm serves as the foundation of a song. In general, you should record the bass and drums first since they guide the other instruments through the song. You may use a different instrument (e.g. acoustic guitar) if the song doesn't need bass or drums.

3. Record the Harmony – Once the rhythm is set, you should proceed by adding a chord structure. That means you should use a piano, horn, synth, or rhythm guitar, depending on your song.

4. Record the Melody – Many songs form the melody using different types of instruments. When recording a song, you should record the dominant parts first (i.e. e.g. vocals, lead guitar, etc.). Once the main melodies have been recorded, you can improve the musical piece by adding the supporting melody.

5. Add Some Color–To finish the song, you need to add those little things that give flare and color to the track. Here are some examples: piano fills, percussion fills, background vocals, and sample sound effects.

How to Record Vocals

This section of the book will provide you with tips and techniques on how to record great vocals.

The Five Problems That Can Ruin the Vocals

- Sibilance – When a person pronounces "f" and "s" sounds, the mouth expels an air blast called "sibilance." Sibilance creates a high-frequency sound. In general, you won't detect this during normal conversations. However, it becomes obvious when the vocalist's mouth is near the microphone. You may solve this problem in two different ways:
    ◊ By using computer programs such as "de-essers."
    ◊ By using the pencil trick. Here's how: Get a pencil and place it over the mic's diaphragm. Secure the pencil's position

Overdubbing:

using a rubber band. With this trick, the pencil splits the air blasts into two and diverts them to the side.

- Foot Noise – Sometimes, each footstep can be heard throughout the whole studio. When the vocalist taps his feet, vibrations will travel up the microphone stand and into the audio recording.
    - ◊ You can solve this problem using a "shock mount." A shock mount isolates the stand and the microphone, thereby stopping the vibrations from affecting the recorded music.
- Popping – When a person pronounces "b" and "p" sounds, he/she expels a powerful blast of air from his/her mouth. You don't notice it during normal conversations. However, during a recording, these blasts of air hit the microphone's diaphragm. This situation creates a punchy and low-frequency sound called popping.
    - ◊ You can fix this problem by using a pop filter. A pop filter creates a barrier between the mic and the vocalist. Basically, this barrier catches the air blasts and allows the singer's voice to pass unaffected. This barrier prevents singers from moving too close to the microphone (which they often do).
- Poor Room Acoustics – If your recording area has poor acoustics, your vocals will be disappointing. Make sure that the acoustics of your studio

matches the songs you are trying to record. This topic had been discussed in an earlier chapter.

- Proximity Effect – In general, microphones produce a low-end boost when a sound source is placed near the mic's diaphragm. This effect is advantageous if you are using an acoustic guitar. However, it can be annoying when you are recording vocals. You can solve this problem in two different ways:

    ◊ By using a pop filter. This will secure a proper distance between the microphone and the sound source (i.e. the vocalist's mouth).

    ◊ By using omnidirectional microphones – These mics are designed to prevent the proximity effect.

The Proper Microphone Techniques

Here are four techniques that you can share with your vocalist. Using these techniques, he will notice significant improvements in his sound.

1. Control the Volume Using Distance – He should move the mic closer as he sings softer and further as he sings louder. This technique will equalize the volume fluctuations, greatly reducing the compression needed in the editing stage.

2. Use the Proximity Effect – A singer may add a sense of intimacy to his tone by moving the microphone close to his mouth during the song's delicate parts.

3. Control Breath Sounds – A vocalist may prevent the undesirable breath sounds by turning his head to the side during each breath. This technique will minimize (or eliminate) the awkward sounds that must be edited later on. However, there are times when the vocalist must breathe into the mic intentionally. This trick can add a beautiful effect for some types of songs.

4. Prevent Sibilance and Popping – A vocalist can prevent these problems by adjusting the distance and angle of the microphone from his mouth. If he knows how to get the proper angle and distance, you won't have to use a pop filter anymore.

How to Record Musical Instruments

This section will teach you the recording methods particularly used for home studios. It will discuss 5 common instruments, namely: bass guitar, drums, acoustic guitar, electric guitar, and keyboards.

For Bass Guitars

When recording a bass guitar, you may simply place a microphone against the guitar box. Here are the things you have to consider when working on this instrument:

1. Don't use standard dynamic microphones – You should record bass guitars using bass microphones. These mics are designed for low-frequency musical instruments such as bass guitars.
2. Use a direct box that matches the song's bass style – Active bass styles require passive direct boxes. Passive styles, however, require active direct boxes.

For Drums

This instrument poses difficult problems when being recorded in a home studio. When recording drums, you usually need:

- Different kinds of equipment – This may involve stands, several microphones, input channels, etc.
- A large recording area – The space should be large enough for all the equipment you need. The room should have great acoustics if you want to record excellent sounds.
- Acoustic/Physical Isolation – This will help you to record the "drum noise" without provoking your neighbors.

Since the things outlined above are often expensive, you may use:

1. Virtual Drums – Nowadays, virtual drums can create amazing tracks. This is because each sound sample used in the software was played by a professional drummer, inside a professional studio, using a world-class drum

set. That means these drums may sound better than real ones (depending on the skills of your band member). Basically, you should go for virtual drums when working inside a small home studio.

Here are two of the best virtual drums currently available: Steven Slate Drums and Toontrack EZ Drummer 2.

2. Electronic Drum Kits – This kind of instrument offers two distinct advantages: (1) an AI module that is better than most virtual instruments and (2) a realistic hardware that can convince you that you are using an acoustic drum kit.

For some people, electronic drums are the best option when it comes to home recording studios. Here's why:

- Good electronic drum kits produce excellent sounds.
- They allow you to record each drum onto a different track, similar to acoustic drum sets.
- You will have a wide selection of drum kits.
- They are quieter than acoustic drum sets. That means you may record without annoying other people.

3. Acoustic Drums – These are the drums you normally see in concerts and music videos. Professional musicians consider these as the best drum sets available today. As they say, nothing beats the "real thing." Here are

some of the things you have to consider when recording acoustic drums:

- The Microphones: You should use dynamic microphones for the drums. For cymbals, however, you need to use condenser microphones. If you don't have a microphone collection yet, here are great mics for each part of a normal drum kit:
  - ◇ Toms – Use a Sennheiser e604. If this one is not available, you may use standard dynamic microphones.
  - ◇ Snare – Use a Shure SM57. If you don't have one, use a standard dynamic mic.
  - ◇ Kick – Us an AKG D112. If you don't have this, you may use any bass microphone.
  - ◇ Cymbals – Use a pair of condenser microphones.
  - ◇ Hi-Hats – Use a Shure SM81. If you don't have one, use a condenser microphone that has a small diaphragm.
- Microphone Positioning – Here are some of the best strategies regarding mic positioning:
  - ◇ For kick drums – You should use two microphones. One of the mics should be in front of the drum; the other one should be in the back. This trick will help you to capture the clicks and thumps of the beater.

- ⬦ For snare drums – Use two microphones: one at the top and one at the bottom. This positioning allows you to catch the rattles of the snare and the cracks of the drum.
- ⬦ For cymbals – You may use two microphones: one for the ride and one for the hi-hat.
- ⬦ For toms – Place individual microphones in front of each drum. Alternatively, you may use a pair of stereo microphones for the toms.
- ⬦ For individual drums – Place the microphone right along the drum's rim. The mic should be pointing downward, as near to the drum's head as possible. Make sure that the microphones do not get in the musician's way.

For Acoustic Guitars:

Acoustic guitars are known for their simplicity. They don't require special tools or cables to produce beautiful music. However, acoustic guitars are one of the most complicated instruments when it comes to music recordings. Aside from the notes, the sound of an acoustic guitar involves:

- The fingers touching the strings
- The palm tapping the guitar's soundboard
- The hand muting some of the strings
- The strings touching the frets and the fingerboard

Sometimes, you have to observe all those details during a recording session. Here are some tips and methods that can help you record this kind of instrument:

1. Use an acoustic DI – In general, home recording studios have less-than-ideal acoustics. You may solve this issue by recording with an acoustic DI instead of a mic.

There are two notable differences between acoustic DIs and standard direct boxes. These are:

- Acoustic DIs offer a high-end sound system that can capture the high-frequency tones of an acoustic guitar.
- Acoustic DIs have a high input impedance that can match the outputs from piezo-electric pickups.

2. Recording with a microphone – If you are satisfied with the acoustics of your home studio, you may proceed with the recording using a "tried-and-tested" microphone. Here are some tips that you can use when recording with a mic.

    ◊ Use a condenser microphone that has an omnidirectional pattern. This type of microphone is ideal because:

        * Condenser microphones are superior to dynamic ones in terms of capturing high-frequency sounds.

Overdubbing:

> * Omnidirectional microphones are superior to cardioid mics in terms of capturing wide sources of sound.

3. The Positioning – This aspect is easy and simple. First, place the microphone about one foot away from the acoustic guitar. Make sure that the mic is pointing toward the instrument's 12th fret. Make some small adjustments in distance and angle until you achieve a great tone.

When working inside great-sounding studios, you may increase the distance between the mic and the guitar. This will help you to catch more studio ambiance. When inside poor-sounding rooms, however, you should move the microphone closer to the instrument. This trick will minimize the undesirable reverbs coming from the studio.

For Electric Guitars

The simplest technique to record electric guitars is:

Place a microphone against the guitar cabinet and hit the "Record" button. However, you can improve the instrument's sound quality with these additional techniques:

1. Record Using a Direct Box – You can plug your electric guitar into a direct box to convert hi-z signals into low-z signals. These low-z signals can be recorded straight into the DAW (Digital Audio Workstation) as a dry material

that has no effects. You may insert an amp simulator into the track to add effects. This simulator serves as the digital version of a guitar rig.

2. "Mic" Your Guitar Cabinet – If you want to have a "professional quality" sound, you have to use a great microphone and a great amplifier. Here are the things you should know:

- The microphone – Lots of people prefer microphones that are designed for guitar cabinets (e.g. Sennheiser e906). However, ribbon microphones and dynamic microphones work just fine.

- The positioning – Place the microphone against the guitar cabinet. Then, make sure that the mic is facing the cone. This is the basic mic positioning for electric guitars. From here, you may experiment with different angles and distances until you achieve a great tone. Alternatively, you may reposition the amplifier itself. Here are three options:

    ◊ Tilt the amp to reduce the phase cancelation from nearby walls.

    ◊ Place the amp on a chair or table to avoid reverbs from the floor.

    ◊ Change the amp's location . . to achieve different sound "ambiance."

- Re-Amp – This is a tool that gives you the sound of an authentic guitar amp and the flexibility of an amp simulator. It works by changing the line-level outputs of your interface into guitar signals that are returned to the amplifier.
- Re-Amps offer two advantages, which are:
    ◇ It allows you to compare and/or blend the "actual" and "simulated" versions. Thus, a re-amp helps you to find the optimal tone.
    ◇ It allows you to tweak the amp's tone and re-record the song even without the presence of your guitarist.
- Here are two great Re-Amps that you can use: (1) Radial Reamp JCR and (2) Radial ProRMP.

For Keyboards

A keyboard is a digital instrument. Thus, you can control and record it easily. Professional musicians claim that keyboards are simpler than those instruments that require a microphone. Here are two simple methods of recording a keyboard:

1. Using Virtual Keyboards: A virtual keyboard, when used with a MIDI (Musical Instrument Digital Interface) controller, provides a powerful recording solution. This is because:
    ◇ Virtual keyboards are generally cheaper than digital pianos.

- ◊ Virtual keyboards provide excellent editing features. That means you may improve poor performances.
- ◊ These keyboards allow you to modify tones at any part of the mixing stage.

For these reasons, if you don't have a great keyboard or keyboardist, a virtual keyboard can help you greatly.

2. Using Stereo DIs: If you have a real keyboardist and a great keyboard, you surely want to exploit those resources by recording the analog outputs directly. However, most keyboards have line connections that produce high outputs. These outputs usually clip when saved using a standard microphone channel. For this reason, you should connect your keyboard to a direct box (just like a guitar).

Remember to use a stereo direct box since the outputs of keyboards are stereo. Here are two of the best direct boxes for keyboards: Radial JDI Duplex and Radial ProD2.

Editing the Music

When recording songs, you should always think about the music editing stage. If you ignore this stage, future overdubbing will be compromised. Simply put, the quality of your songs will be ruined. The editing stage involves lots of critical decisions. Excessive editing may result in cold and lifeless tracks. Insufficient editing, on the other hand, may lead to chaotic and sloppy-sounding tracks.

This chapter will explain the basics of music editing. In addition, it will help you make excellent decisions for your audio recordings.

What Does "Music Editing" Mean?

Music Editing is defined as a process that modifies the original output of a performance. It involves certain techniques such as punching, sampling, stretching, compressing, splicing, flying, etc. Basically, these techniques are used to modify the pitch, timing and tempo of a song.

The Process

The amount of editing you need depends on the quality of the sounds you have recorded. The better the sound quality, the less editing time will be required. The editing stage will be a walk in the park if you will concentrate on the musicians' performances during the recording/overdubbing stage.

All of your editing work must follow the process explained below. This process involves three steps, some of which may be unnecessary, depending on the quality of your recorded tracks. The process will help you to stay organized throughout the editing stage. It will stop you from rushing things.

You may approach this 3-step process in two ways. First, edit the track step by step and work on everything as detailed as is required. Second, work on the track as a whole and edit it while focusing on the "big picture." Many music producers prefer the second approach since it greatly helps in preventing excessive editing.

To help you understand this process, everything will be explained as if a vocal performance is being edited. You should study this example carefully since vocal editing involves lots of details. Once you understand how the process works, you may apply it to any instrument or musical performance.

First Step: General Editing

This step involves identifying the best materials from what you currently have. If you have 5 recordings, you should begin by identifying which of the recordings is best. That recording will serve as the basis for the rest of the editing stage. Then, check if there are better parts of the track in the other recordings. For instance, the 2nd recording has a better verse, the 3rd recording has a better bridge, and so on. Keep going until you have the best sections from all the recordings. Edit your chosen track by adding the parts from other recordings.

Once done, listen to the edits you made. Check if the song sounds believable and coherent. You might need to adjust levels between the edits so your judgments are not affected by minor differences (which are purely technical). Identify the parts that require more work before moving on to the next step of the process.

Second Step: Medium Editing

You will only reach this step if you are still not satisfied with the song. While conducting the first step, you will notice that there are some words, sections, or phrases that need more editing. If you wrote some notes about those problem areas, start working on them one at a time.

If the situation permits, start this step by editing entire phrases. Focus on the feel and attitude rather than perfect pitch when evaluating the quality of the song. Remember that a minor pitch correction on an excellent performance will sound better than a mediocre performance that has perfect pitch. If you have to get some words from other recordings, make sure that the end product still has a natural feel and timing.

You may "copy-and-paste" performances from the earlier parts of the recording. This trick is required if you are not satisfied with the existing performances for that section. For instance, you may copy the guitar solo at the beginning of the song and use it for a later section. However, you need to ensure that the melody and timing are still natural. Use the older version as a guideline when checking the timing and melody.

If possible, don't use a single performance for more than one part of the song. It would be better if you will grab another performance from a different recording. This trick will help you to keep the minor differences that happen from one part to the next. Basically, it will make your listeners feel that they are listening to a "live" performance.

Third Step: Fine Editing

You must listen to the entire song prior to starting the fine editing step. While listening, don't focus on the vocals. Rather, listen to the combined result of all the recorded parts. You won't be able to concentrate on the important aspect – the overall emotion – if you will simply listen to the vocalist's performance. Many artists, producers, and sound engineers have been too focused on the vocals they don't notice that the "big picture" is being ruined.

This behavior often turns an energetic recording into a plastic surgery situation where the song sounds great, but somehow feels wrong. Keep in mind that the minor "imperfections" influence the song's authenticity. Thus, these "subtle flaws" play an important role in the overall music experience.

Choose your problem areas. Work on the obvious problems first. Avoid the "work from the start" strategy where you will edit everything thoroughly. You should always focus on the song's overall feel. Some recordings require this kind of heavy editing to bring out the song's core message. For instance, if you are working on a rap song about being a fierce fighter, you have to perform heavy editing to achieve the needed effect.

Mixing the Music

The mixing stage is perhaps the most complicated part of the music recording process. In general, music producers have a hard time mastering the art and science of music mixing. This is the reason why music mixers earn large amounts of money by doing their job. Recording companies know that music mixing is a critical part of the recording process. Thus, they are willing to pay for sound mixers who can perform the job well.

This chapter will provide you with tips and techniques that you can use for mixing your audio recordings. The information you will find here applies to home recording studios.

The Basic Music Mixing Procedure

First Step: Levels & Panning

During this step, you should position the sounds (e.g. bass, drums, vocals, etc.) so that they complement the song. If you want to focus on one aspect (e.g. the vocals), the rest of the sounds should be arranged in a way that they highlight your chosen aspect. For example, if one or more of the instruments are "out of position," listeners won't be able to focus on the vocals.

In general, you should start with the major aspects first (e.g. bass and drums). Most sound engineers prefer to mix these aspects before working on the rest of the song.

Second Step: Subtractive EQ & Editing

This step focuses on removing the unnecessary stuff. At this point, you will filter off the low-frequency hisses and rumbles, mute sound parts that cloud the recording, apply subtractive techniques to indistinct songs, and edit out the silent sections.

You will receive tremendous benefits from this step. It lets you enjoy the beauty of each musical performance. Since you will remove the "garbage," you will be able to manipulate the sounds according to your preferences.

Third Step: Compression

This step affects the size and volume of a sound. In general, compression is used to:

- Level out performances
- Add more presence to some performances
- Manage the groove and sustain of the performances
- Reduce the size of the performances

Fourth Step: Effects Processing

The effects and reverbs you use during the mixing stage determine the size of the recording. Identify what size is best for the kind of music you are working on. Often, classical songs sound "below-average" when stored in a tiny space. Punk rock tracks, on the other hand, sound like a huge mess when placed in a large space. Remember that the decisions involved in this step depend on the kind of music you are recording.

Fifth Step: Shaping EQ

During the mixing stage, you have to know where you incorporate EQ into the recording. You have to decide which instruments will be dominant; these instruments require most of the frequency areas. For instance, the bass guitar requires low to midrange frequencies to sound good (way much higher than kick drums). Here, you may remove the "lows" and "mids" (i.e. the frequencies) from a kick drum and add them onto the bass guitar to achieve more warmth for the latter.

You should master this "give and take" principle of handling frequencies. You may mute or isolate them to create TV mixes, instrumental mixes, and A Capella mixes.

Sixth Step: Grouping Instruments

The mixing stage involves different kinds of grouping. Nowadays, many music producers use the "mix grouping." This kind of grouping allows you to alter the mute status or sound levels of the entire group by altering the mute status or sound level of one of the members. However, you should use this grouping only if your song's sounds and balances are close to what you want.

There is another type called Audio Grouping. Here, you will "bus" (i.e. place in an internal path) the whole group into a stereo track so that you can process the group in its stereo form. This grouping offers some advantages. These are:

- It allows you to process large groups of instruments.
- It allows you to create mix stems.
- It allows you to generate simple variants of a single mix.

Seventh Step: Automating the Mix

You should adjust the mixing levels after each stage of processing. This trick will ensure that the sound levels are even throughout the song. During the mixing stage, however, there will come a time when you should automate the fader levels to accommodate the changes in the different sections of your recording.

Nowadays, musicians do not perform the entire song in a single recording session. The songs are typically recorded according to the stages outlined in this book. That means the musicians that work on overdubs simply respond to the recorded materials. Overdubbing musicians tend to make subtle pulls and pushes that don't match the song at all.

This results in a recorded performance that is full of poor dynamics. You have to adjust the dynamics based on what is happening in the recording. In this situation, automation will help you to fix the inconsistencies quickly and easily. The finished product is so smooth you won't believe that the song's parts were separately recorded.

Here's How to Apply Mix Automation

1. The General Levels – Make sure that these levels are perfectly balanced.
2. The Section to Section Levels – Ensure that all of the song's sections have balanced sound levels.
3. Combining the Performances – Once you are satisfied with the overall sound levels, it is time to weave the recordings together. At this point, you have to make sure that the dominant instruments can be heard clearly.
4. The Polishing Stage – Here, you should work on the song's subtle nuances. These nuances add life to the recording so make sure that listeners can hear them.

Eighth Step: Recording the Final Mix

This is the final phase in the mixing process. Once you have decided to "print" the song, you need to work on the separate mix stems. You can work on these mix stems easily. In fact, you can send them to your remixers who may want to get the instrument groupings. Since the effects and the level automation are burned onto the mix stems, your remixers won't have to waste time in recreating the vibe of your mix.

Mastering the Recording

This chapter will explain the process of music mastering for home recording studios. It will also give you practical tips and techniques that can help you with your tasks.

The Process of Mastering Songs

This process involves a sequence of stages that have been followed by musicians for decades. The process itself has retained its main characteristics. However, three things have changed: (1) the tools and techniques used, (2) the medium musicians work with, and the (3) final output is now released to public consumers. Although these aspects have changed, the basic stages of the process are still the same. These basic stages are:

1. Preparing – Make sure that the final mixes are saved in a workable format.

2. Transferring – Nowadays, file conversions (i.e. analog to digital) are no longer required. If you are working on CDs or downloadable files, you may transfer the analog ones first. Here are some of the things you need to consider during this stage:

    ◊ Bit depth

    ◊ Sample rate

- ◇ The quality of file converters (if applicable)
- ◇ The quality of the digital clocking source you used.

The four things listed above will help you to retain the quality of your original mixes.

3. Ordering – Many sound engineers import tracks in the order specified for the album. However, you sometimes need to import songs in a different order because of technical reasons (e.g. the source only works for limited tracks). Once you have transferred the songs into your mastering program, you may make changes in the song order without affecting the editing process.

   If you are mastering tracks for CDs, the song order must be based on the general flow of the CD. You should start the CD with a powerful track, but not necessarily the one that you will release for promotions and radio plays. Keep in mind that you have to spread out the good songs in the entire album. Your listeners won't make it to the end of the CD if you show all of your best singles early on.

4. Editing – You have to edit the beginning and ending of each song to make sure that the transitions are clean. Often, you should leave a few seconds at the start of a track and use a fade-in. This trick will help you to smoothen out the transition from utter silence.

5. Spacing – This aspect defines the flow of the CD from start to finish. During the mastering stage, you need to identify the natural entry points for every song. You might need to add a longer pause after a heart-pounding song if the next one has a lighter feel. Conversely, you should minimize the space after a soft song if the next track is "hard-hitting."

6. Processing – Here, you should use compressors and equalizers. Compressors are often used to add more power and level to the mixes. Equalizers, on the other hand, are used to increase the depth and clarity of a mix.

7. Leveling and Coding – When mastering songs, you have to ensure that the overall sound levels from track to track are consistent. This aspect may pose serious difficulties to inexperienced sound producers. For instance, you need to have a good ear to perfect the compression and density of frequencies for the entire album.

   The coding process allows you to enter CD Text, Copy Protection Info, ISRC Codes, and UPC/EAN Data into a CD or digital file (e.g. mp3). This process also involves the ID tags used to identify the song.

8. Dithering – This process helps in preserving the quality of high-resolution tracks. Here, low-level noises are added to the track while the bit depth is being lowered from 24 bits

to 16 bits. The lowering of the bit depth is required when mastering CDs.

9. Creating the Final Recording Master – This is the final step in the mastering process. Here, the sound engineer will generate the final recording master. The mastering process creates two types of outputs: (1) PMCD files and (2) DDP files. PMCDs (Pre-Mastered CDs are created specifically for manufacturing plants.

The DDP (Disc Description Protocol), on the other hand, is a file that holds all the necessary data for the production of the glass master (i.e. a glass disc that is layered with a thin film). This glass master is then used for the creation of the CDs you see in music stores.

Conclusion

Thank you again for downloading this book!

I hope this book was able to help you to learn the basics of setting up a home recording studio and recording your own songs.

The next step is to practice your craft and enjoy the beats that you create.

Finally, if you enjoyed this book, please take the time to share your thoughts and post a review on Amazon. It'd be greatly appreciated!

Thank you and good luck!

Rake

Other Related Books

Songwriting 101 (2nd Edition):
Inspiration, Tips, Tricks, and Lessons for the Beginner, Intermediate, and Advanced Songwriter
http://goo.gl/EYFBKa

Songwriting–Crafting A Tune:
A Step By Step Guide To Songwriting (2nd Edition)
http://goo.gl/QvqtNn

Home Recording: An Introduction To Home Studio Recording In The 21st Century
http://goo.gl/7aA9qL

Photo Credits

"Microphone" by Matthew Keefe
(No changes were made to this photograph)
https://creativecommons.org/licenses/by/2.0/legalcode
https://www.flickr.com/photos/mkeefe/2349283746

"KRK Rokit 6 Review" by Dave Dugdale
(No changes were made to this photograph)
https://creativecommons.org/licenses/by/2.0/legalcode
https://www.flickr.com/photos/davedugdale/12142931716/

" 1,2,3 ready go! (Line 6 Tone port)" by captain.orange
(No changes were made to this photograph)
https://creativecommons.org/licenses/by/2.0/legalcode
https://www.flickr.com/photos/10527553@N03/5122895556/in/photostream/

" Mic screen" by Danny Ayers
(No changes were made to this photograph)
https://creativecommons.org/licenses/by/2.0/legalcode
https://www.flickr.com/photos/danja/5440593933/

Printed in Great Britain
by Amazon